DRAW
PIRATES

Then Write a Story

Stephanie LaBaff
Illustrated by Tom LaBaff

Enslow Elementary
an imprint of
Enslow Publishers, Inc.
40 Industrial Road
Box 398
Berkeley Heights, NJ 07922
USA
http://www.enslow.com

Library of Congress Cataloging-in-Publication Data
LaBaff, Stephanie.
  Draw pirates in 4 easy steps : then write a story / Stephanie LaBaff ; illustrated by Tom LaBaff.
      p. cm. — (Drawing in 4 easy steps)
  Includes index.
  Summary: "Learn to draw pirates and sea creatures. Also, write a story about them, with a story example and story prompts"—Provided by publisher.
  ISBN 978-0-7660-3839-4
  1. Pirates in art—Juvenile literature. 2. Drawing—Technique—Juvenile literature. 3. Sea stories—Authorship—Juvenile literature. I. LaBaff, Tom. II. Title. III. Title: Draw pirates in four easy steps.
  NC825.P57L33 2012
  741.2—dc22
                              2010054010
Paperback ISBN 978-1-4644-0012-4
ePUB ISBN 978-1-4645-0462-4
PDF ISBN 978-1-4646-0462-1
Printed in the United States of America

092011 Lake Book Manufacturing, Inc., Melrose Park, IL

10 9 8 7 6 5 4 3 2 1

Illustration Credits: Tom LaBaff

To Our Readers: We have done our best to make sure all Internet Addresses in this book were active and appropriate when we went to press. However, the author and the publisher have no control over and assume no liability for the material available on those Internet sites or on other Web sites they may link to. Any comments or suggestions can be sent by e-mail to comments@enslow.com or to the address on the back cover.

♻ Enslow Publishers, Inc., is committed to printing our books on recycled paper. The paper in every book contains 10% to 30% post-consumer waste (PCW). The cover board on the outside of each book contains 100% PCW. Our goal is to do our part to help young people and the environment too!

Contents

Getting Started

Lots of Paper →

Pencil Sharpener →

Your imagination ↘

I ♥ 2

← Pencil

Eraser ↙

ARTIST'S SURVIVAL KIT

Drawing pirates and ships is as easy as 1, 2, 3, 4! Follow the 4 steps for each picture in this book. You will be amazed at what you can draw. After some practice, you will be able to make your own adjustments, too. Change a pose, move an arm, or draw a different sword. There are lots of possibilities!

Follow the 4 Steps

1 Start with big shapes, such as the head and neck.

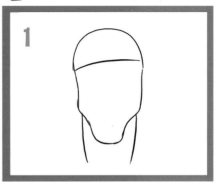

2 Add smaller shapes, such as the eyes, nose, and mouth. In each step, new lines are shown in red.

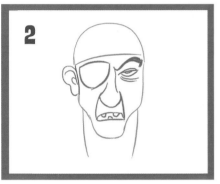

3 Continue adding new lines. Erase lines as needed.

4 Add final details and color. Your pirate will come to life!

Pirate Pete

1

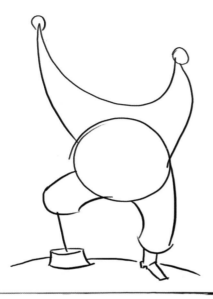

2

Erase the dotted lines under his sleeves.

3

Erase the dotted lines under his hands.

Go crazy with the hair!

4

6

Dashing Dave

1

2

Erase the dotted line under the shoulder.

3

Erase the dotted lines
under his sword.

4

Isn't he dashing?!

Eyepatch Ed

1

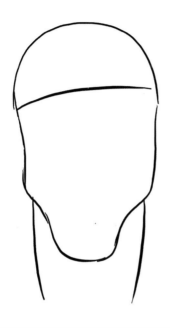

2

3

4

8

Ghost Pirate

1

2

3

4

Spooky!

Harry Hook

1

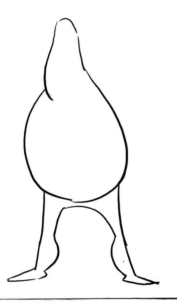

2

Erase the dotted lines behind Harry's coat.

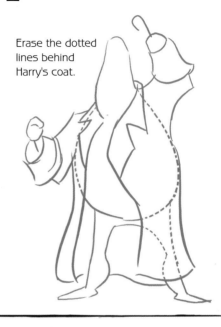

3

4

Lady Lavina

1

2

Erase the dotted line under her clothes and on her hands and arms.

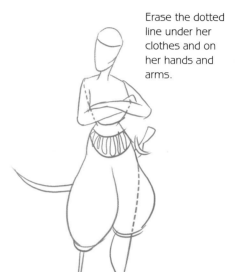

3

Erase the dotted lines on her shoulders.

4

Spyglass Sid

1

2

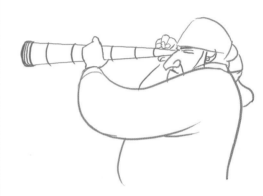

3

4

Siren

1

Use curvy lines!

Fish-like body.

2

Erase the dotted line at her waist.

3

4

Skeleton

1

2

3

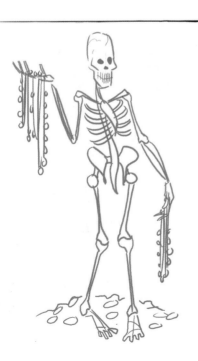

4

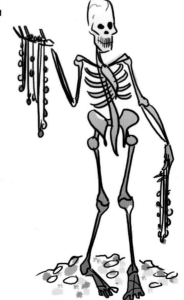

Monkey

1

2

Erase the dotted lines behind the arm and leg.

3

4

Sword

1

2

3

Add some horizontal lines to make the blade look shiny.

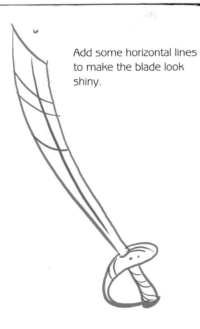

4

Skull Sword

1

2

3

4

Dagger

1

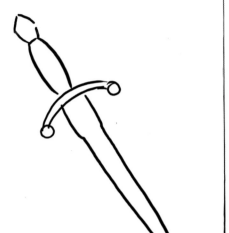

2

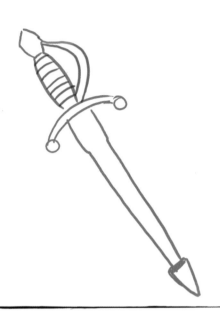

3

4

Pistol

1

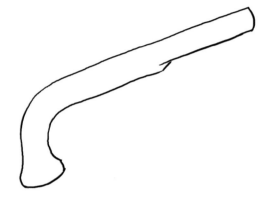

2

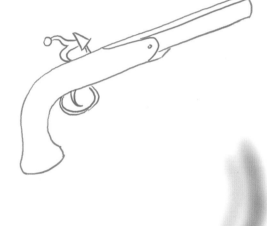

3

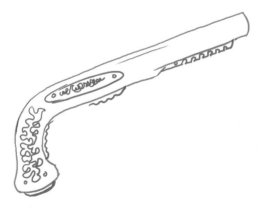

4

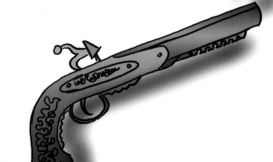

Cannon

1

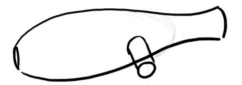

2

Erase the
dotted lines.

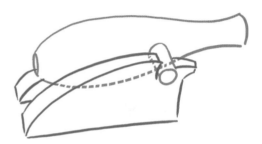

3

4

Seagull

1

2

Erase the dotted lines behind the beak.

3

Erase the dotted lines behind the headband.

4

Anyone got a french fry?

Shark

1

2

Erase the dotted
lines behind the
fins.

3

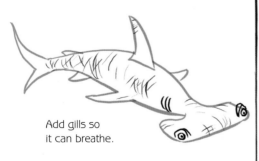

Add gills so
it can breathe.

4

Map

1

2

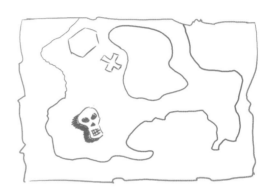

3

4

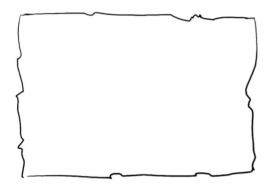

Jolly Roger

1

2

Erase the dotted lines in the corners.

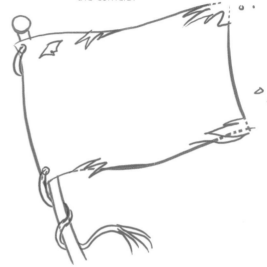

3

4

26

Treasure Chest

1

2

3

4

Compass

1

Find two cups to help make circles.

2

Now, put a dot in the center and grow some leaves.

3

4

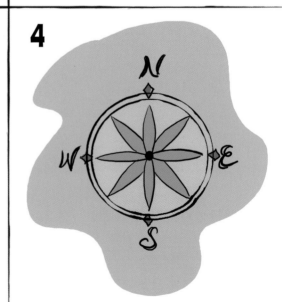

Powder Keg

1

2

3

4

29

Crow's Nest

1

2

The pole is in the middle, so erase the dotted line behind it.

3

4

Palm Tree

1

2

3

Okay, take a deep breath and SKETCH in the leaves!

4

Not too shabby!

Rowboat

1

2

3

4

Stormy Seas

1

Time for an
easy one!

Small waves are back here.

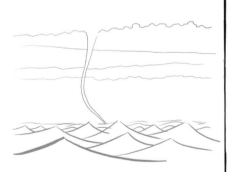

Big waves are close.

2

3

4

Pirate Ship

1

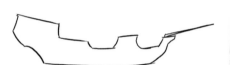

2

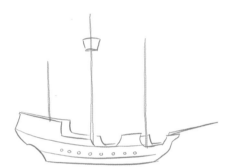

3

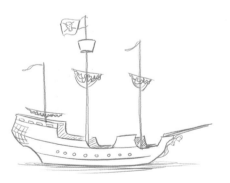

4

Skull Island

1

2

3 Add birds to show how big Skull Island is.

4

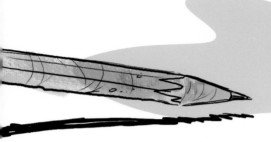

How to Write a Story

Write a Story in 5 Easy Steps

Are you ready to write a story to go with your drawings? Maybe you have a story you want to illustrate. Follow these five simple steps to make your very own story with drawings.

Step 1:   *Prewriting*

Do you want to write about pirates? Maybe you have an idea for a story about pirates attacking a ship. Keep in mind the drawings you want to use and base your story around them.

One way to begin your story is to answer these questions: Who? What? Why? Where? When? How?
For example:
Who is your pirate?
What happens to him in your story?
Why is his story interesting?
Where and when does he live?
How does he react to his situation?

Here is a good brainstorming exercise:
Fold a paper into six columns. Write the
words *Who? What? Why? Where? When?*
and *How?* at the top of each column. Write
down every answer that comes into your
head in the matching column. Do this for
about five or ten minutes. Take a look at your
list and pick out the ideas that you like the
best. Now you are ready to write your story.

Pirate Story Starters

One day I was walking down by
the docks . . .

The ship appeared out of nowhere . . .

I was digging in the backyard when
all of a sudden . . .

We'd been at sea for two weeks when
we finally spotted land . . .

The ship was under attack . . .

The storm came up suddenly . . .

"Walk the plank!" the captain ordered . . .

The pirate ship sank near Dead
Man's reef . . .

Step 2: Writing

Use the ideas from the list you made in Step 1. Write your story all the way through. Don't stop to make changes. You can always make changes later.

A story about a pirate sleeping in a hammock isn't very interesting. What could happen to this pirate? What if there were a pirate ghost on the ship? Think of all the trouble a ghost could stir up. Your story will be more exciting if you don't make things too easy for the pirate.

Step 3: *Editing*

Read your story. Is there a way to make it better? Rewrite the parts that you can improve. You might want to ask a friend or teacher to help. Ask them for their ideas.

Step 4: *Proofreading*

Make sure the spelling, punctuation, and grammar are correct.

Storyboarding

It's time to see how your story works with your drawings. Find a table or other flat surface. Spread your drawings out in the order that goes with your story. Then place the matching text below each drawing. When you have your story the way you like it, go to Step 5. You can pick a way to publish your story.

Step 5: Publishing Your Book

You can make your story into a book.
There many different forms your book can take.
Here are a few ideas:

 Simple book – Staple sheets of blank paper together along their edges.

 Folded book – Fold sheets of blank paper in half, then staple on the fold.

 Hardcover book – Buy a blank hardcover book. Then write your finished story in the book, leaving spaces to add your art.

 Bound book – Punch a few holes along the edges of some pieces of paper. Tie them up or fill the holes with paper fasteners. There are many fun and colorful binding options at office supply stores.

Digital book – Create a digital book using your computer. There are some great programs available. Ask an adult to help you find one that is right for you.

Our Story

You have finished the five steps of writing and illustrating a story. We bet you created a great story! Want to see ours? Turn the page and take a peek.

The Ghost Pirate of Skull Island

The pirate ship raced through the stormy seas, headed for Skull Island. Pirate Pete wasn't thinking about the raging waters, though. He turned and saw Lady Lavina's ship in hot pursuit. "Drat," he mumbled. Lady Lavina, his mortal enemy, had been trying to steal his treasure map ever since she found out about it.

Suddenly, Spyglass Sid called from the crow's nest, "Land ho! I spy Skull Island to the starboard."

"Finally!" thought Pirate Pete. "The treasure will soon be mine." But at that moment, something swooped out of the sky heading straight for Pirate Pete. As he held up his arms to protect himself, he felt something being ripped out of his hands.

"Noooo!!!" He watched as Lady Lavina's parrot flew back to her ship with the map in its beak.

Pirate Pete's ship sped to the island and the crew rowed to shore. They spotted Lady Lavina's ship a short distance away.

"Get them!" ordered Pirate Pete. Off they ran, swords and pistols drawn, toward Lady Lavina and her crew. But just as Pirate Pete and his men were about to attack, they stopped in their tracks. Standing in front of them was the most terrifying pirate they had ever seen.

"It's the Ghost Pirate!" someone whispered. Everyone knew the legend of this ghost. Years ago, he had been stranded on the island as he searched for buried treasure. He had died without finding it, and he haunted the island to this day.

"Who has the treasure map?" he moaned. Lady Lavina, who was holding the map, ran at him with her sword, but the Ghost Pirate stopped her with one bony hand. He plucked the map from her grip.

"Into Skull Dungeon with you!" The ghost tossed her into the dark, skull-shaped cave, never to be seen again.

The men ran back to the ships, relieved by their narrow escape. As they sailed away, Pirate Pete looked back and saw the Ghost Pirate floating away. The ghost would finally have the treasure he had been dying to find.

Further Reading

Books

Cowell, Cressida. How to Be a Pirate. New York: Little, Brown Books for Young Readers, 2010.

Harpster, Steve. Pencil, Paper, Draw!: Pirates. New York: Sterling, 2007.

Levy, Barbara Soloff. How to Draw Pirates. New York: Dover Publications, 2008.

Long, Melinda. How I Became a Pirate. New York: Houghton Mifflin Harcourt, 2003.

Matthews, John. Pirates. New York: Simon & Schuster, 2006.

Index

Internet Addresses

PBS Kids. Dot's Story Factory.
<http://pbskids.org/storyfactory/story.html>

Scholastic.com. Writing Games.
<http://www.scholastic.com/kids/stacks/games/>
Click on "Writing Games."